The Democratic Asylum

By keith rauh

ISBN:9781081167370

DEDICATION

This Book is dedicated to the silent majority.

CONTENTS

ACKNOWLEDGMENTS

This book is a tribute to the American People and the silent majority. It's a reflection of myself and my personal views.

CHAPTER 1.
THE BEGINNING OF THE END!

When I was young, I never really followed politics. This would all change in 2015, when Donald J Trump announced his candidacy for president. The democrats believed that their candidate was the anointed one and was a sure bet to win the election and give them a third term of Barack Obama. They would find out in 2016 that was anything but reality. I knew when our now president came down the escalator, I was looking at the next President of the United States of America. I was in a small majority!

All the polls were showing that Mr. Trump had no chance of ever being elected. We would later find out that polling data didn't even come close to matching up with reality. There was a silent majority and they were going to speak loudly. Each campaign rally that was held had record numbers of attendees. The media quickly caught onto this anomaly and began nonstop covering them. They weren't doing this to accurately report the news, but to report on what was said as it shocked them, and they couldn't believe some of the things a presidential candidate had the audacity to say. This was the beginning of the end of political correctness for millions of Americans and it couldn't have come soon enough.

The media and the democrat party started to take notice of the campaign promises and tactics used by Mr. Trump and began their attack on him, his character, and the growing number of supporters he was gaining. He was bringing in new people to politics in record numbers which would later prove to be part of a winning strategy. The republican party shock was growing because an outside came in, hijacked their party and wasn't worried about the traditional tactics used by the media and the democrat party to take down candidates in the past.

It was a contentious primary fight ultimately leading to Donald Trump taking down 16 highly qualified candidates and winning the republican nomination for president. This would of course piss off many of what are now known as the never trump caucus and lead them to employee tactics only previously used by people on the left. Fortunately for most republicans once the nomination was secured, they would fall in line and put party over personal opinions. They had a new goal at this juncture, to beat one Hillary Rodham Clinton, the democrats anointed candidate with no real challenger except, Bernie Sanders and his democratic socialism. They knew that with her record she could never be president, although very few people thought she was going to lose.

The democrats believed that their candidate was the anointed one and was a sure bet to win the election and give them a third term of Barack Obama. They would find out in 2016 that was anything but reality. I knew when our now president came down the escalator, I was looking at the next

President of the United States of America. I was in a small majority!

All the polls were showing that Mr. Trump had no chance of ever being elected. We would later find out that polling data didn't even come close to matching up with reality. There was a silent majority and they were going to speak loudly. Each campaign rally that was held had record numbers of attendees. The media quickly caught onto this anomaly and began nonstop covering them. They weren't doing this to accurately report the news, but to report on what was said as it shocked them, and they couldn't believe some of the things a presidential candidate had the audacity to say. This was the beginning of the end of political correctness for millions of Americans and it couldn't have come soon enough.

The media and the democrat party started to take notice of the campaign promises and tactics used by Mr. Trump and began their attack on him, his character, and the ever-growing number of supporters he was gaining. He was bringing in new people to politics in record numbers which would later prove to be part of a winning strategy. The republican party shock was growing because an outsider came in, hijacked their party and wasn't worried about the traditional tactics used by the media and the democrat party to take down candidates in the past.

It was a contentious primary fight ultimately leading to Donald Trump taking down 16 highly qualified candidates and winning the republican nomination for president. This would of course piss off many of what are now known as never trump crowd and lead them to employee tactics only previously used by people on the left. Fortunately for most republicans once the nomination was secured, they would fall in line and put party over personal opinions. They had a new goal at this juncture, to beat one Hillary Rodham Clinton, the democrats anointed candidate with no real challenger except, Bernie Sanders and his democratic socialism. They knew with her record she could never be president, although very few people thought she was going to lose. She spent over a billion dollars and still couldn't take down a true outsider of the political game. Mr. Trump was out financed but he was not going to be out witted. He used social media to an even greater extent than Barack Obama to reach the masses and register record numbers of Republicans and Independents. People who were never interested in politics or had lost hope long ago would suddenly come out from every corner of America.

The Forgotten man and woman, as the future leader of the free world called them, were listening and the rest of the world would soon be listening. As a candidate and even to this day, he has found a way to use twitter to reach the masses and control daily news cycles and the narrative of the week. Let's not take this for granted though, the media tends to take his tweets outs of context and turns them around, so they can use them against him. Daily they will use the same old identity politics play book they have been using since at least the 1960's. What was once a two to four-year campaign strategy is now a daily attack on our presidents' character. He is called a racist, homophobic, xenophobic, a misogynist, a sexist, a rapist and even a pedophile. All these accusations are from the truth as he is an equal opportunity offender. He does not see people differently based on race, religion, color, creed, nationality, sexual identity, gender or any other class of people democrats use to pander to voters.

The democrats have long been using the power of division politics to win votes. If our president sees any thing that makes us different its simply their political party. The media will try to portray him as the divider and chief but, his policies bring us closer together based on patriotism, love of our country, and economic values. The democrats cannot let us be unified on these principals because they know united, we stand, but divided we fall.

Democrats have long known that divided people to achieve votes will gain them votes but this strategy isn't working as it once had. They want everyone to be treated equal but separate people based on their differences. They need to stop using this play book because we are all part of one race, the human race. The democrat party, the media, and many liberal democrats don't only hold this disdain for the president, they also have it towards anyone who supports him. In 2015 face book also was about to go through a fundamental change. Originally it was used as a way for people to connect with family members, old friends, play games and pretty much tell people what you were doing on daily basis. This all began to change in 2015 when Mr. Trump secured the republican nomination for president. People suddenly were sharing political posts in massive numbers.

People started to lose interest in what was going on with their friends and family and became hyper focused on politics. Even now politics is the subject that dominates social media. This also changed the way people got information, we no longer only got our information from the mainstream media, but we were getting it from many sources including candidates them self. We were also able to share our own opinion instead of a media narrative they wanted us to follow. People were finally able to say what was on their mind, and they could even say it in their own way even if people didn't like the way they said it. The days of political correctness were coming to end, unfortunately freedom of speech didn't fare so well. Like any thing that is controlled by someone else, the owners of social media sites quickly caught on and started their mission to silence people who had different points of view than them. If you didn't conform to this group think or you didn't agree with their view, they found ways to silence you.

If companies held certain religious beliefs, they would reach out to the masses to boycott your company. They felt if they could hurt you economically then you would subscribe to their views. They also did this to conservative talk show hosts by attacking their character in order to get advertisers to cancel commitments with their network. Of course, they originally only used these tactics against republicans and conservatives but as time went on, they used some against companies they supported. They even used these tactics against a supreme court nominee and almost destroyed his life. In that instance they said you should blindly believe his accusers, but when the shoes on the other foot they get a free pass. This isn't always true because if you don't conform to their group think and you on their side of the aisle, they will eventually turn on you too. You must fall in line or they will eat you alive one way or another.

Fortunately, they would learn for a lot of Americans, we were not buying this way of thinking any more. We were making up our minds and we were determined to win, and we would win. All the polls were saying Donald Trump had very little chance of winning the 2016 election but internal polling in the democrat party must have told them other wise This brings us to the greatest coo attempt in the history of the United States. We wouldn't learn this information to much after the election, but the democrats decided they had a plan, they worked with the democrat national committee, a foreign national with intelligence connections, and paid to secure propaganda from people who were likely Russian propaganda agents working for the Russian government. They new they had to stop Mr. Trump anyway possible. They eventually leaked this propaganda to the media, which in turn lead to counter intelligence investigations, and FBI surveillance of the president's campaign staff, family members and others. They had now used a circular mis information strategy to make it look like the president was working with a foreign government. They wanted to beat him so badly and knew they couldn't do it on the issues, that they were going to take him down in any way possible.

This leads us to the leader ship at the FBI, they had bias that would later come out that revealed there was a deep state working against a presidential candidate and would stop him at any cost. They couldn't afford to have an outsider come in and turn the government upside down, but that is exactly what he did. If Mrs. Clinton had won the presidency no one would have known this information, it simply would have disappeared like her emails.

This has taken us a little farther ahead than where we were. Most of this was going on behind the scenes and wouldn't be revealed until after a 2-year multimillion-dollar government investigation. An investigation, democrats would hang their head on for over two years in hopes it would reveal an impeachable offense to allow them to remove the dually elected president from office. It did exactly the opposite, it confirmed to millions of Americans that the president was the true patriot he claimed to be.

The democrat and media used a lot of different strategies to prevent the election of Donald J Trump, but they all failed. They woke up on election day 2016 with great hopes of electing the first women president, and shattering some imaginary glass ceiling but they would soon learn they had chose the wrong woman.

Early in the day both sides were anxious but confident at the same time. The democrats thought it would be an early night, and the republicans weren't sure but knew it all rode on some key battle ground states. No one predicted how late this election night was going to go. As the night when on and results came in, people were starting to go in to shock. The media couldn't believe what they were saying and refused to see it till they knew it was over.

The so-called election experts had their calculators out to determine electoral votes and the percentages of how likely it was Mr. Trump would win. The numbers early said he had zero chance of winning, but you could see as time went on and his percentage to win went up these people were going into shock. They couldn't fathom from their studio bubble how Americans could vote for this candidate. They tried to process and analyze it, but it just didn't add up to them. Time after time they said how he ha to win certain states or he couldn't reach 270 electoral votes.

Normally election results come in quickly but for some reason it was well into the night and no one was predicting the winner of the election. They were holding on to hope that maybe, just maybe, it wasn't going to turn out the way it inevitably did. Very early the next morning it had finally become official, we knew who the 45th president was and what was to come next was unpredictable.

CHAPTER 2.
THE END OF THE BEGIINING

Early the next morning we finally knew who had won the election. For the Trump supporters this was relieving as they could finally go to bed. They would analyze this more in the morning when they woke up. The other side wasn't so lucky. They had to process what happened immediately. What was planned on being the victory celebration of the century was quickly becoming an impromptu therapy session. There was shock in their facial expressions, and of course the media would plaster it everywhere. This was the story no one ever expected.

The losing side waited for their leader to come out and give a speech, but this didn't happen. either she was in shock, drunk, or couldn't stay up that late due to whatever health problems she suffered during her campaign. The people soon would break down into tears and would be screaming in the streets in an epic melt down. No one on the left could believe what they had just experienced. I'm pretty sure therapists and counselor offices booked an increased amount of appointments over the next couple weeks. This was the incarnation of what is now known as Trump derangement syndrome, a term used by conservatives to describe the inability to except the results of the 2016 presidential election. Of course, this isn't a real mental health diagnosis, but it someday may very well be one.

A lot of people have trouble accepting things, but this was a new extreme we hadn't seen yet! They say ever since mental health hospitals and institutions closed, we have an unchecked mental health crisis. The 2016 election proves this to be accurate. Fortunately for most, it can be managed with therapy and medication but for some they are going to an outrageous extreme. A group that already existed by the name of Antifa, was now going to use tactics we haven't seen in many years. They were going to resort to violence and intimidation tactics to silence their opponents, they use similar tactics to Nazi Germany all while claiming they are against fascism and silencing free speech. They are really a domestic terror organization and even use masks like the KKK, in a ploy to hide their identities. They really should be labeled by the government as a terrorist organization but to this day that hasn't happened yet.

For the two and a half years since the election, the media has also tried to silence their critics and use every accusation they can to stop President Trump from being successful. The coverage of this president has been over ninety percent negative and they rarely report the positive things he is doing, or the great economic news. We experience record low unemployment, high GDP numbers, and even have reformed criminal justice laws, but if you watch certain networks you will never hear about these things. The president has an incredible ability to reach the masses though. He uses his rallies to inform people of all the accomplishments he has achieved and what he wants to do in the future. The media tends to cut off his speeches and rallies when he starts reporting all the good things that are happening. This is one of the reasons he has deemed them the fake news media, as well as the exaggerated stories they report daily

The American people ae smarter than that though, all though some will blindly believe the media no matter what they report. These are the same people who need a warning on a hot cup of coffee telling them the beverage they just bought is hot. Common sense isn't all that common in the information and technology age. A wise man once said you can't fix stupid, and he was 100 % right. For these people the numbers still don't add up, maybe it has something to do with common core math or maybe they just can't accept reality anymore.

The media empire doesn't have the power they once did now that the social media age is upon us. Advertising revenues must be way down as those funds have been transferred to social media advertising, as it has a far greater reach than traditional commercials. Mrs. Clinton had over a billion dollars for her campaign and was still unsuccessful at winning. Mr. Trump found a way to win with way less money but a far greater reach, he had mastered the art of the campaign as an outsider. His experience in television and business marketing may have played a great role with this. Traditional television ads for political campaigns and issues is no longer as effective as it once was because people don't watch television like they used to. With the introduction of sites like Netflix, Hulu, and other on demand ways to access programs people really don't watch live or prime time television any more, unless they are news buffs like myself.

We are quickly approaching the 2020 election and if the large number of democrat candidates want to win, they are going to have to find a way to reach out to people which can compete with a sitting president who has accomplished many things in less than three years. A billion dollars and the most recognize candidate in history couldn't do it, so they are going to need to get creative beyond the insane ideas that they come up with daily. Reaching the masses with ideas that are manageable or will send our country backwards or using identity politics are all losing strategies. They are also going to have to stop attacking each other with the same tactics they have traditionally used against republicans. They are eating each other alive with tactics I call democratic cannibalism! If for the entire democrat primary season, they work to take each other out, it will make it easy for President Trump to win reelection. He will only have to hold rallies and speak directly to the American people about his accomplishments, of which there are many.

Starting in 2015 politics has forever been changed. The political world takes top priority and many aspects of people's lives. It hasn't just invaded social media and television news rooms and studios, it has also taken over pop culture. Washed up stars with no career prospect have come out of the wood work to gain attention and possibly drum up prospects for new ventures. Even singers like Madonna and actresses like Ashley Judd have made threats against the white house. If this was an every day American like you or me, we would have been paid a visit by secret service and likely charged with a crime. This takes us back to the Trumped-Up false accusations many of these people make daily. One relatively unknown actor by the name of Jessie Smullet even went as far as staging a fake hate crime against hi self. It's believed he did this to extort additional income from his employer the fox television network and to make the trump supporters look bad.

There are no lengths to great for these famous people to go to. The big media empire, the democrat party, social media websites, newspapers and people of pop culture are going to great extent to create a smear campaign against the president and his supporters. They continuously reported on how the Russian government spent money on ads to create division in America, but they did the dirty work for them, the Russians didn't need to use propaganda to divide us, our very own institutions in America already had done it. The part they overlook though is we may have differences of views and opinions, but we will always be more united they can ever divide us. The media for a long time has profited off things like racial divide, attacks on police offices and spreading hate, but only a limited number of Americans buy this anymore. I am starting to think the media knows there days are numbered, as times keep changing and technology advances. After over two years of spreading a fake narrative about the president, their own viewers started leaving in record numbers, either because they lost hope, or they switched networks. It's likely it's the later as their ratings tanked when it was proven to be a false narrative and their viewers lost hope in them. Their ratings plummeted and the fox news empires ratings for news and opinion shows sky rocketed.

This may be the beginning of the end for some networks we will see in time. If they do go out of business or get bought out by other networks, they will not have any one to blame but them self. We can only hope they will become fairer and more balanced and go back to reporting the news instead of spreading a narrative and their opinions as if it were actual news. Only time will tell what is to come for them, their viewers and television in general. America is counting on them to become objective, but it doesn't look promising. Even educational institutions like colleges, universities and public schools are trying to program people to believe a certain way, fortunately for us there are still freedom fighters, investigative journalists, and people who are willing to fight to get the truth out.

CHAPTER 3 THE CENTRIST.

The media has long relied on polls and polling data to predict the out come of elections, but since 2016 this data is becoming ever more in accurate. The polls in most cases was totally wrong, except in few outliers that show who had won each republican primary debate as well as the general election debates. Pollsters and people who studied polling data for many years are losing credibility and their days like the media may be numbered. This may be a result of how polls are conducted. Polls are often over sampled with people who support the pollster's point of view or based on political party affiliation. These polls are usually conducted including people who are considered reliable voters. In 2016 there was anomaly of voters that hadn't voted in years or were going to be first time voters. When most of these polls came out people didn't believe their accuracy because they all were stating that no one was polling them. Only time would tell what was really going to happen.

There was ever growing number of people registering to vote and they were going to determine who the next president of the United States of America was going to be. A lot of political strategists believe that the far left or the far right determine election, but we know that to not be reality. Elections are not won by people in each political party. Elections are won by swing voters and people in swing states. These voters tend to be independents and not affiliated with any political party at all. They have all the power and they shift elections. These same voters are part of the silent majority as they aren't often used for polling data.

Independents are an interesting group because they believe in both conservative and liberal values. They are not progressives and they don't vote based on extremes. They also don't vote based on identity politics. They vote based on issues that reflect their views and issues that matter in their personal lives. They likely hold conservative views on economic policy but are more liberal on social issues such as legalization of marijuana, gay marriage and even open plural marriages. They are patriotic Americans who salute the flag not burn it, recite the pledge of allegiance, believe in national security, and putting America first over the interest of the rest of the world. President Trump seized on that in his campaign and still does to this day.

They believe in helping veterans and the homeless people in America over foreign nationals trying to enter the country illegally. They tend to be the voters who vote based on economic issues such as jobs and unemployment. Over the past several decades they seen their jobs shipped over seas as a result of poorly negotiated trade deals. These are the people who believe made in America is more than a slogan. It is sense of pride. This same group of voters also seen fulltime employment decimated after the affordable care act due to regulations involved in it. They were no longer able to work one full time job, but in many cases had to work two or three part time jobs. They were also losing health insurance, forced to change their doctors and were punished for not having health insurance. One of the plans of the democrats is to provide free health insurance to illegal immigrants even after punishing them with a fine for not being able to purchase health insurance due to the higher premiums and deductibles under the affordable care act. This was known as the individual mandate, it is another reason president Trump was able to win and he has since eliminated this provision from law, likely deeming the entire affordable care act unconstitutional.

These voters were seeing fundamental changes to the nation they loved. It was becoming unrecognizable to them and they weren't going to stand for it. The democrat party was going as far left as any one has ever seen before, they were trying to institute socialist policies and even subscribe to an open borders policy that mirrored how the European union worked. Most Americans have enough commonsense to know it's dangerous to have an open unchecked border and it could lead to another terrorist attack.

The media tries to vilify these voters and supporters of the president claiming these are extreme views and down right racist and xenophobic. This couldn't be any farther from the truth. That is just the media and the democrats using their outdated identity politics play book again. It's one of the few campaign strategies they have. Most Americans who lived through the attacks on September 11th, 2001 know exactly why immigration reform, and border and national security are important. They don't ever want another 9/11 style attack to happen again.

The independents are a different breed of voter. They believe in law and order and enforcing our laws. They support law enforcement and won't stand for the media vilifying them. They believe immigration and asylum laws need to be changed and adjusted to support a 21st century world. They also know we can't be the entire worlds savior. We can't be the world's welfare state, it is unsustainable, and our national debt will not allow it. They believe in the principals put forth by our founding fathers such as we are all equal and should treated as such. They believe in freedom. They also believe these principals apply to legal citizens and don't apply to people who came here illegally or over stayed their visa.

The democrat party continues to get more extreme every day and haven't realized their policies aren't in touch with most Americans but especially the independents. The independents look deeper into the issues and how policy will affect their life and what the consequence of legislation will do in the long run. They don't take things at face value and to tend analyze them on a far deeper basis.

The media continues to take these voters for granted. They try to vilify them by insulting them and accusing them of being bigots and racists all while ignoring the fact, these are the people who elected president Trump and are likely to get him reelected. A wise scholar once said it's the economy stupid. He was 100 % correct and people are going to vote based on the economy as they almost always do. The media is promoting the democrats and their crazy ideas of how to make America a better place, but all they are really doing is working to get the president reelected. This may be their plan, because the coverage is non-stop about the president now, if he were to lose reelection, they wouldn't have much to cover except failed policies of the democrats and how they really aren't going to help the American people.

These independent voters likely have contributed to the decline in ratings and viewership of most of the main stream medias channels. People are wise and won't stand for being treated like fools who are supposed to believe the lies they are being told. Part of the reason the media hates president Trump so much is because he tells the American people the truth and he does it in a way that every day Americans understand and relate to. He doesn't sugar coat things and he will say them in a nonpolitical correct way, that people from certain circles can't relate to.

They don't talk the way he does, and they can't understand how anyone can. They are appalled by his way of talking. The independent voters and normal people do talk that way. They are tire of being looked down on and thought less of because they are not like the people they see on the news and in holly wood and educational institutions. Even the upper cholent of the federal bureau of investigation had this same kind of hatred for them. They said things in text messages like they could smell them at Walmart. These text messages have also revealed their insurance policy against them and their plan to elect president Trump. They must have seen who was going to win t he lection long before he did. They were willing to do almost anything to stop him and his supports and the independent voters and people who were centrists.

What is now known as the deep state and their attempt to start a coo of the duly elected president is finally starting to come out although we will likely never know the full extent of how far it went. They used to call these same voters' conspiracy theorists when they came up with these kinds of accusations and beliefs that things like sleeper cells for terrorist could exist in America. We are all aware government corruption exists but none of us had any idea how far, how high, and how deep into the government that really goes. For some people like former secretary of state Hillary Clinton we will never know. She destroyed too much evidence and government officials have worked to cover it up so no one will ever know except those involved.

CHAPTER 4
INMATES OF THE ASYLUM

Let's introduce you to the 2020 candidates for the democrat nominee for president of the United States of America. We will start with their front running candidate and the person who is polling highest so far. Former senator and the most recent vice president Joe Biden. I will start by saying he is the perfect example of a swamp rat, a person who spends most of their life in politics and public office. Although there are quite a few controversies which should have ended his career long ago, and if he had been a republican likely would have. To put this in prospective he has been in politics since America first landed on the moon, that is longer than I have personally been alive. If democrats choose him to be their nominee, it will likely be one small step for man and giant leap off a cliff for the democrat party.

Democrats often talk about their party being the party of diversity, but their top two candidates are older white men, a class of people they are usually against. Democrats also often talk about treating women with respect, but this candidate has done everything from smelling little girls' hair to kissing and hugging older women and other people's wives. If he was a republican, he likely would have been charged with sexual harassment or even worse sexual assault for some of the things he has done Dome of his opponents have even accused him of racism in the most recent primary debates. He has always been the king of the gaffs and made many mistakes when speaking in public. He was also totally unprepared for attacks against him in the debate and even ended rapped up his time on his own totally making himself look like a fool and a weak candidate. Maybe he is just rusty, but he sure doesn't look like he could handle dealing with other world leaders.

Next, we will discuss the 2nd place candidate in poles. A self-proclaimed democratic socialist. The funny part about that is he is usually an independent and not even a democrat. He was the first to introduce the policy of Medicare for all in the 2016 primary against Hillary Clinton. Almost all the candidates have adopted this position, or some other form of universal government run health care. That is except for the front runner who believes in revamping the affordable care act. He even mentioned the same lies they used prior to the law passing like you could keep your doctor and healthcare plan if you liked it.

In Bernie Sanders failed 2016 run for office he campaigned on reforming trade deals which is a policy the present president has. President trump is working to reform and renegotiate these deals. This candidate has since dropped any mention of these ideas from his campaign. He also used to run on increasing taxes on millionaires but once news got out that he was a millionaire, he suddenly changed it to billionaires. This may have also been a swipe at president trump as he is a billionaire. One of his main policy proposals is to raise the minimum wage to $15 dollars and hour an amount he calls a living wage. The problem with that is his own staff recently pointed out that they don't make this much money and they demanded he pays it. If you're going to campaign for a policy, you better practice what you preach. The on main down fall despite all this may very well be the fact that he is almost 80 years old and white man.

Now we come to the candidate known as the Rockstar of the group. One Beto O'Rourke aka Robert Francis O'Rourke. He was a little-known Texas congressman until he decided to run for the senate seat held by Ted Cruz. He lost this bid. He used the nick name Beto to appear hipper and to appeal to the Hispanic population in Texas and across America. Let's remember the 2016 primary where Ted Cruz lost to now president Donald Trump. This makes me wonder why he thinks he would have a chance in the general election against the president if he couldn't beat a senator who already lost to him in the last primary.

Why he has been deemed the rock star of the group is beyond me. He originally had gained popularity, but his poll numbers and attention have quickly faded when the next candidate I will talk about entered the race. Some of his great claims to fame were social media posts at the dentist, getting a hair cut and campaign event where he was standing on the counter of a restaurant where people eat food. In my opinion he is not presidential material.

Next, we will get into a group of senators. We will start with a couple minorities and the democrat's candidates of diversity, California senator Kamala Harris and New Jersey senator Corey Booker. These two candidates gained their claim to fame in the confirmation hearing of now Justice Brett Kavanaugh. They totally attacked his character to gain attention for their presidential candidacy and the 2020 presidential campaign season hadn't even began. Mr. Booker even channeled his inner Hollywood by claiming he was having a Spartacus moment. Mrs. Harris furthered her cause recently by attacking front runner Joe Biden on racial issues to pander to African American voters.

Next on the list is Massachusetts senator Elizabeth Warren. A person president Trump has nick named Pocahontas because she used her alleged native American heritage to enter schools and gain an advantage in her life. She later would take a DNA test that would reveal she had less than one percent of native American in her blood line. She is still being drilled on her issues with honesty because of these claims. She is quite progressive and campaigns on policies like raising minimum wage and waging war on wall street and banks as well as the wealthy. The reality of that is in the over six years she has been senator in my own state she has done almost nothing.

Next, we have senator Tulsi Gabbards and former Colorado governor John Hickenlooper. These two candidates are quite moderate for the democrat party now and should be polling higher than they are. The reality is the democrat party has gone to such an extreme they just can't gain any traction. If they are going to gain any ground, they are going to have to come up with some attention-grabbing publicity stunt or work hard in the next democrat debate to gain favor with the American people.

Our next candidate has been gaining ground until just recently. The South bend Indiana mayor Pete Buttigieg. He is the first openly gay presidential candidate in American history and he makes sure the country knows this. He has received negative press recently for his failed attempt at handling an officer involved shooting of an African American suspect. If he was unable to handle this situation, he is going to struggle with world leaders like Putin and Kim Jong Un. The last group of candidates are a group I have deemed the nobodies. They can't poll higher than one percent and California congressman Eric Swalwell has already dropped out of the race. These are the candidates who are most likely going to run out of money quickly. None of them have name recognition except one billionaire business man Tom Steyer who is trying to copy President trump by being a billionaire business man and political outsider although he has been a major democrat donor for years.

CHAPTER 5
THE POWER STRUGGLE

I society since the beginning of time there have always been power struggles. Two things have always controlled societies, greed and power. The more money you have the more power you will likely acquire. This is even more true   when it comes to political power. Elections for years have been won by who spent the most money to get elected, at least up until the 2016 presidential election when President Trump managed to outsmart his opponent with quite a bit less money despite being a billionaire.

The biggest cancer on a political party   is division with in its own ranks. This showed true a few years ago for the republican party with the inception of the tea party caucus. they weren't the only part of the party to be divided as moderates, conservatives and more liberal members also showed division. to the point where even journalists noticed and wrote an obituary for the party. We all have now witnessed president Trump single handedly use social media to resurrect the party from the dead and except for a few never trumpers bring unity back to the party. The party is now unified on economic, national security, and most social issues. They support patriotism and the principals laid forth by our founding fathers in the constitution.

The democrat party isn't so lucky to remain unified. For years the media talked about how united they were and that republicans would never win if they remained united. I'm sure speaker of the house Nancy Pelosi wishes that was the case, but the division is growing and its growing quickly. The long serving members like Pelosi and senator Chuck Schumer are losing power to the up and coming freshman which are controlled by special interest groups and worse than that they are controlled by social media.

The democrat party was once supposedly the party of the working man, but they have gone more and more to a socialist party and farther and farther left. The newer members are quickly pushing the party to a party of handouts and free bees. They used to be about labor laws and fair wages and commonsense health care. They used to be about protecting Americans. Unfortunately for the leader ship the party is quickly becoming the party of social justice, illegal immigrants, and handouts for everyone. They believe in high government mandated wages, high taxes, free college, and even free healthcare for illegal immigrants. Sadly, they have no way to pay for any of these ideas except raising taxes, but the price tag is higher than any tax increase they could ever pass. These younger members think they can wave some magic wand and fix all of Americas problems.

One of the ideas they came up with was a

plan called the green new deal. This plan was a real fantasy, it included eliminating air planes, raising taxes, killing cows to end cow flatulence. They tried to sell it as climate saving bill but its really about government control of every area of our lives. Bernie Sanders tried to revamp his socialist policies by calling it democratic socialism. Despite his creative way of classifying it, it's still the same old socialism that has failed in every country it's been instituted in. No matter what way they try to sell it, it's about controlling people. Ideas often sound good on the front end but when you dig deeper it tends to come with a lot of stipulations and ways to keep people dependent on the government. If they can keep people dependent on the government, they gain more control of them and their lives.

It is becoming more and more aware that speaker Pelosi is only speaker of the house in name. She is not the leader of the democrat party any more. She is likely only a figure head much like Robert Mueller was for the investigation named after him. He apparently didn't take part in his own investigation as his recent congressional testimony made everyone aware of this fact. This no more obvious then in press conferences where she must state how the party is unified and she's in control when everyone knows the part is deeply divided.

The speaker continues to be questioned about impeachment, but she keeps dodging these questions. There are several factions now inside of the democrat party. We start with the moderates who campaigned on health care and won in pro president

Trump districts. They made promises to fix healthcare but don't support fixing the affordable care act nor believe in socialized medicine such as Medicare for all or a single payer government run health care system. They are party members who would be more likely to work with the president on this specific issue. They are in a vulnerable position as they will have tough reelection battles if they don't get something accomplished in the next year.

Next, we have the impeachment crowd. They are going to spend every waking moment between now and the 2020 election to keep the impeachment talking point alive despite recent loses they incurred from the Mueller report and congressional testimony he provided. They will issue subpoena after subpoena requesting documents, they know they can't be provided like secret grand jury materials. They will also seek testimony from president trumps lawyers and family members despite this already having been investigated for over 2 years. Despite knowing even if they brought up a vote in the house of representatives and it passed it would-be dead-on arrival in the republican controlled senate. This would just be another loss for them and cost them even more support from people in their party. There real goal is not to impeach the president but to keep a never-ending issue until the 2020 presidential election. If they keep pushing this, they are likely to lose control of the house of representatives effectively giving republicans a majority to pass president Trumps agenda.

The third group we have in the democrat

party is socialist freshman wing. They have a large following on social media but very little support in congress. Their key legislative plan called the green new deal didn't even get any support in congress. No moderates wanted to be connected to that outrageous plan. These are the social justice warriors of the party, they believe in free health care for illegal immigrants, $15 an hour minimum wage, on demand abortions up to, and in some cases after birth abortions. They even believe government dollars should fund these abortions. They support open borders and eliminating our nations sovereignty, border protections, immigrations and customs enforcement and even home land security, the very people who protect us from terrorists and other national threats. Most of their plans are not supported by the American people and they have low poll numbers. They are likely being controlled by social media and special interest donors who want to fundamentally change America. The saddest part of this is they are pushing almost all the 2020 presidential election contenders farther and farther left. Another issue they support is taxing people up to almost ninety percent of their income in some cases.

In public they try to show a united party between these factions of the party as well as with the moderates. One recent instance where they were unified was a procedural impeachment vote that only got votes from ninety-five members of their party. The more divided the party becomes and the farther left and unrealistic their policies get the easier it will be for president Trump to win reelection, the republicans to take back control of the house of representatives and gain even more seats in the United States senate. If your conservative or even moderate, you must shake your head at some of the ideas they have or come up with on a weekly basis. Just when you think it can't get any worse, they always find a way to go even bigger and even more insane. Todays democrat party wouldn't be recognized by most of our grandparents and great grandparents.

This same group of young freshman democrat also have a great hatred for the president, his supporters, and quite likely America. They continuously make accusations of racism while they themselves will make racist statements. One of them even went as far as to say the government should profile white men, which is the textbook definition of racism. She made false claims that white men or likely to be radicalized than actual terrorists and claimed they kill more people than any one else which is based on no facts or statistics.

Another area they focus on in their speeches, and social media posts is about ending gender specific words and pronouns. They believe that words like man kind and man hood or even man hole should all be changed to some non-gender specific wording like human kind. This doesn't shock me as they believe either there are 63 genders or no gender at all despite science proving this to be untrue. They apparently only believe in unproven climate science but not biology.

Some of there other wonderful ideas are to eliminate plastic straws and plastic bags. What they missed with that is most of the waste they find in the ocean comes from five various Asian countries and not the United states. It is at the point now where businesses are removing straws and providing adult sippy cups like toddlers use. This is kind of appropriate considering they cry like children and throw temper tantrums when they don't get their way. Plastic straws are only the fifth most common item found in our oceans and cigarette butts are number one. Also getting rid of the straws doesn't do very much considering the entire cup is made from plastic as well as many other items we package products in. One thing I have noticed they haven't tried to ban are e cigarettes which are disposable and contain a ton of plastic as well as chemicals which I'm sure are way worse for the environment than plastic straws.

The reality is if the democrats don't find a platform they can promote and unify behind, and Americans can support they are headed for major losses come November 2020. They have some serious soul searching to do at this point and if they don't dig deep it will be a long time before they win another election anywhere. Americans want law and order and common-sense policies that benefit American citizens not craziness and chaos. They want their interests to be put first over other countries and illegal immigrants.

CHAPTER 6
POLICY PRESCRIPTIONS

The democrat party is going to an extreme not many people will soon be able to recognize. If they were able to come up with some common-sense realistic policies, the republican party would be more than happy to work with them on areas where they can find common ground. The first area I suggest they come to together would be social security reform. They could eliminate the salary caps on social security and allow social security to be taxed on all income not just up to the 130,000 dollars it presently is collected on. This would   make the program much more sustainable for many years to come. Next, they can make a policy where if you retire with over 10 million dollars you can no longer collect social security retirement benefits. The money collected from the taxes they pay would go back into the system and be used for younger worker retirement benefits as well as for social security disability programs. There is no reason multi-millionaires and billionaires should be collecting government benefits.

The social security disability and ssi programs

could also use some improvements. One aspect where it need improvement is in the actual application process. The government needs to stop relying on doctors who likely never meet an applicant or an independent contracting doctor who meets an applicant for 30 mins to an hour one time. They need to give precedent to the doctors who work with the applicant on regular basis especially mental health professionals who have long established record with the person who is applying for benefits. The next area is in how they deny people for benefits. They are using the physical ability of a person to do simple job-related tasks but not taking in to account other things that may affect their ability to perform on a regular basis at a job that requires very little skill. Some examples are concentration, memory, ability to focus and mental health conditions. They also use a vocational expert who only knows if these jobs exist n the national economy but not locally and they often base their decisions on government statistics. The next problem with this is the government tend to be reactive in stead of proactive. These same jobs they use to deny people benefits are quickly being replaced by technology and will eventually no longer be available to lower skilled workers. They could also consider that a person who has done heavy physical work their entire life isn't as likely to be able to transition to another skill set and may develop chronic pain further affecting their ability to perform any job.

We also need to be aware that ton of money is being sent to foreign countries. This money is untaxed and a lot of it is coming from government programs. All money sent out of America should be taxed at drastic rate between forty and fifty percent. The money raised from this tax can go to border security and immigration enforcement. It is ridiculous this is even allowed to happen in the first place, it is unchecked and unregulated and could very well be financing drug cartels or terrorists. This needs to be addressed as soon as possible

Next, we can institute common sense annual minimum wage increases based on the GDP. Most government mandated programs have increases based on cost of living increases not some random number politicians pull out of their ass. Democrats are calling for fifteen to twenty dollar an hour minimum age but that drastic of an increase would stifle the economy, cost jobs and reduce hours of workers. It would likely also increase the trend of replacing legal workers with illegal immigrants who work for less money. If we increase minimum wage by two to four percent annually the increases would be gradual having less affect on business. In states where the minimum wage is already hire it wouldn't affect them at all as their wage is already set at a higher rate. These gradual and annual increases would benefit Americans more than one giant increase every 20 years. This would also kill republican's argument that minimum wage increases shouldn't happen at all as its gradual and would have very limited effect on businesses and the economy.

Another common-sense policy that both parties can agree on would be legalization of recreational marijuana. Unfortunately, big pharma has a lot of lobbyists who are fighting to stop this from happening as it would cut into their profit margins. Eleven states have done this already and more than half have legalized medical use. This is the same way alcohol prohibition ended, one by one, state by state. We can place a ten percent federal tax on sales and dedicate those tax dollars specifically for mental health treatment. The legalization is inevitable, so we might as well use it for something positive.

Now we will dig into immigration reform and border security. The first thing we need to do is eliminate the ninety-day fiancée visa. If you unfortunately watch the reality show ninety-day fiancée like me, you will understand this program is being abused drastically. If someone wishes to marry an American citizen, they can immigrate based on their own merit not simply for marriage purposes. We also need to do a raid to round up all the people who have over stayed their visas. We can give them an opportunity to resolve their issues or they will get deported. We must be firm but fair when it comes to immigration matters. We also need to strengthen our asylum laws and reduce the number of refugees as we cannot take on the entire world's population.

We need to work tirelessly to secure our border an continue building a border barrier to prevent illegal immigration, drug smuggling, human trafficking, and terrorism. We need to end daca and other programs that encourage people to come to America illegally. We then need to round up and deport any one here illegally especially criminals and gang members.

We then need to institute a merit-based immigration system and reduce chain migration. We should limit family-based chain migration to a spouse, the immigrants' children. We can make an exception for the immigrants' parents if they are suffering from health problems and the immigrant is the sole care taker. We should admit people based on skills and ability to support their selves financially. Any person immigrating to America should have the resources to take care of them self for two years and not be able to use any government assistance program for at a minimum, five years. All immigrants should be required to speak or learn English. We also should be doing DNA tests to all family units that show up at our border to ensure they are indeed related. If they are not the adult arriving with the child that is not related to them should be charged with human trafficking and then we will do what ever possible to reunite the child with their biological parents.

Let's dig in to healthcare reform now. The best thing we can do is remove the profit margin and stop healthcare companies and big pharma from creating customers and encourage them to create cures. We can start by limiting them to making no more than ten percent profit. Health care really should be nonprofit if you believe it to be a human right as democrats often campaign on, but we will allow them to still make a considerable amount of money. With the money they still make over the ten percent they can then use to fund in the following ways. Thirty three percent will go to fund drug and treatment research as ell as clinical studies. The next thirty three percent will go to funding health insurance programs for the poor like Medicare and Medicaid. The final thirty 33 percent of revenue after the 10 percent profit will go to mental health treatment programs in all public schools. The policies and laws to do with health care that have passed or are campaign promises have done nothing to fix health care, they were and are simply insurance reforms. If we come up with common sense plans like this, we cover both preexisting conditions and will hopefully be able to find cures for cancer, the common cold, the flu and many other diseases. Maybe we should start with the easier ones and work our way up to the more complex especially conditions that effect the mind like brain injuries and mental health conditions.

We also need to address the homeless problem in America. If we address the underlying issues like mental health and drug addiction, we will be able to end homelessness especially for our veterans. The conditions on the streets from homeless people will only lead to more out breaks of diseases we once eliminated. Rampant poverty in our inner cities also leads to health problems like increased cases of asthma and even worse things like typhus. If we can raise people up out of poverty be removing their dependence on the government, we can clean our streets of rats and hypodermic needles. Although the veteran's administration has improved over the last couple years, we need to take this even farther. We need to allow even more choice and options for our great veterans and leave the veterans administration to deal with specialized care.

On a side note to veterans care we need to

modernize and stream line our military. We don't need to just spend more money we need to move centuries ahead of our enemies. We need to start using more robots and drones in military operations instead of having human casualties. If we take technological position to war, we will no longer see soldiers come home with missing limbs and body parts or post-traumatic stress disorder. We need to look ahead to the future and explore space and how it will play a role in the future of war fare.

I'll be brief with tax reform policy. We need to make President trumps tax reform and cuts permanent. We need to allow small business start ups to operate for one-year tax free. We need to reduce self-employment tax down to a much more manageable rate than the thirty 33 % average. We also need to give more tax credits to businesses that invest in creating jobs and expanding their companies. We also need to increase taxes on companies who do business in other countries and give them tax credits for every job they bring back to America.

The last policy I will get in to is infrastructure. We need to improve our roads, bridges, tunnels, pipe lines and electric grid. We need to learn ways to be less dependent on the electric company and become more self-sufficient. Hopefully in the future most of us will live off the grid. We are moving into the next generation of technology we never imagined only 40 years ago. We must advance as fast as or even faster than our technology does. We are developing autonomous cars and planes. Drones will soon be the number 1 method of transportation. We are going to be using 5g communications devices and many things most of us can't even imagine. Robotics will become a major part of all our lives from medical care, to house cleaning, to manufacturing, maybe every aspect of our lives. Our infrastructure is from a century gone by and we need to move it to the next century. This is already apparent in many houses that have smart devices like Alexa or a Roomba vacuum cleaner. In the future everything is going to communicate from traffic lights to houses to businesses and more. It is long over due for us to look forward instead of backward. We need our government to start taking a pro active stance as opposed to a reactive stance.

On one lest side note a good policy improvement would be to reallocate funds from foreign aid to programs that combat poverty, homelessness and hunger. We need our policies to put Americans first over foreign countries who give us very little in return for the assistance we provide them.

CHAPTER 7

REDUCATE AMERICA

It becomes obvious quickly when talking or dealing with someone in our younger generation that we are failing as a nation when it comes to educating our nation's youth. Common core is an epic failure and it shows in the lack of basic skills by todays youth. We need to remove political views, social justice, and other agendas from our once fine nation's educational institutions.

We need to go back to basics and reeducate our children with basic skills of math and English and begin teaching history again, so we can learn from it but not try to erase it. Many groups today are trying to erase our history by destroying statues and murals much like the tactics used by ISIS. Those who do not learn from history are doomed to repeat it which no one wants to happen. We also need to start teaching civics and government in schools again so when our youth reaches adult hood, they will know exactly how things work as well as why something can or can't be done. We also need to remove agendas from colleges and universities and if they don't then we should punish them with removal of federal dollars they receive in aids and grants and subsidies. The federal government should not be financing an agenda. These universities and colleges should also be punished if they don't protect an individual or groups right to free speech as is guaranteed in the constitution.

We also need to start taking a more technological approach to education. We are in the information and technology age and education needs to evolve as we do technologically. We need to place an emphasis on stem education. Science, technology, engineering, and math are the corner stone to our future endeavors.

Not only do we need to focus on these areas, but we need to institute life skills training. When people leave high school, they are ill prepared to deal with life's realities. We need to teach our youth basic skills like cooking, hygiene, how to fill out a check and job applications. We need to teach them how finances work and how to pay bills. Our youth would also benefit from time management strategies and how to act professionally in public and in a job interview. We also need to teach communication skills, so they will know how to interact with others in a proper manner. We have lost respect for authority and family values in our country and we need to work to reinstitute these age-old values.

Other financial areas we need to teach our youth is how accredit rating works, how to build one and how to use it properly as well a how to monitor it to prevent identity theft. The basics are key but there are so many skills that get neglected in public education. Most young adults don't understand how or what it takes to obtain am mortgage, credit card, car loan or even apply for an apartment.

Another set of skills we can work on are health issues. We need to teach proper hygiene. We need to teach them how to take care of them self, how to obtain health insurance and what they should talk to a doctor about. Most importantly in this area we need to teach them basic first aid techniques they can use in an emergency. We should also teach ways they can protect them self from diseases and common ailments like the flu and common cold. Of course, some of these things should wait till high school but others can be taught to even the youngest of children. We should also bring drivers education back into high schools for low or no cost depending on the student's financial ability to pay.

These are just some of the ideas I think could greatly shape our nation's future. There ae many more but it all starts with building a solid foundation. Having a good starting point and building on it will not only benefit the student them self but all of humanity going forward.

Next, we must keep our children informed of all their options. We must stop grooming our children to one option of college. There is an enormous amount of highly skilled jobs that go unfilled every day in America. Not every child will be college material and not everyone wants to end up with massive amounts of student loan debt. We need to bring vocational education back to high school. We need to gear smart kids with a knack for technology to go into trades and apprentice ships. Many career paths which pay well and have on the job training would be a better suit for many of today's youth. Many of the degrees offered at colleges and universities will lead to careers that won't make the actual degree worth it financially in the long run. We need to devote fifty percent focus on college type careers like doctors, lawyers and teachers. We need the other fifty percent to be directed towards skills-based jobs and education to full fill jobs in manufacturing and skilled trades in order to eliminate the skills gap we presently have in America. Many of those jobs pay quite well but this isn't often pointed out.

CHAPTER 8
THERAPY SESSIONS

If we look around America there is one under lying theme we can again and again. There isn't hate per say but there is a growing anger. We see it again and again daily. Its ever present in grocery store checkout lines, in online debates, drive through windows and fast food restaurants. There is a great divide in America and it needs to stop. Maybe it isn't any more common than it used to be, maybe we are just more aware with everyone having a camera and trying to capture the next viral video moment. Then there is always the possibility that maybe we are just paying more attention to it now.

We need to ask our selves why this is happening and what we can do to prevent it from getting worse. A good first step would be to stop focusing on what divides us and redirect our focus on our similarities and what makes us alike. We need to look deep inside of our selves to find out why some else's point of view or actions bother us so much. What is it we see in them that we allow to affect us so greatly to the point we rebel and act out in inappropriate ways in public such as yelling or even worse in a violent manner? When it comes to groups like antifa it is a political agenda that leads them to acting out in this manner. They are going to do whatever it takes to get their point across even if it means assaulting journalist and innocent people.

We can not tolerate or accept this type of behavior or allow it to become a socially acceptable norm. We must think deep and hard before we act instead of reacting. We also need to think about the person we are confronting answer have no idea what a person may be dealing with in their personal life. The reality of it may be that the person is dealing with mental health conditions, may have just lost a family member or a job. They might also be a decorated war veteran suffering from ptsd and you just might set them off to the point they responded in an unpleasant manner to put it lightly.

We must go back to two age old principals. One that united we stand and divided we fall and two the simpler one, love thy neighbor as we love our self. Granted some people hate their self and this may contribute to their behavior as well but still treat them as if they were a family member in need. It might do us all a bit of good to take five minutes out of our day to down load the calm app or some other similar antianxiety app on our phones. At the least it will teach to pause for a few seconds before acting instead of just reacting. Maybe practicing mindful meditation would be good as well. It may not be a bad idea to take a yoga or tai chi class in order to learn breathing and relaxation exercises. Some of us might want to investigate going to therapy a couple times of year even if we don't have an anxiety issue because sometimes having someone to talk to can do a world of good. Sometimes people just need someone to listen to them with out judgement. Maybe you will fight out you have a mental health issue and can start to work on dealing with it and living with a condition you didn't know you even had. I think a lot of people dealing with addiction may very well be covering up or masking other under lying conditions.

For those of you who are religious maybe it's time to say an extra prayer or attend an additional mass or religious gathering. Maybe you can take some time and pray for the other side or those you disagree with. Maybe just pray for America and people's general wellbeing or that we can put aside our differences soon. For those who are simply spiritual and don't subscribe to a certain religious faction you can always ground yourself, mediate or even sage yourself or your home. Some might think this is silly, but any bit of positivity surely can spread without us even knowing it.

CHAPTER 9

AFTER CARE

Going forward need to start being pro active and a lot less reactive. We need to take steps to make sure we act in an appropriate manner no matter what some one else is throwing ta us even if that's literally. We must take time to process what's being thrust upon us and consider how we can act instead of reacting. If some one attack us for our views on the internet we must find a creative way to acknowledge their point of view. Even if they are insulting us, we must act in a way to not further encourage their behavior. In public we must start acting with respect and letting things go. We can't take everything so seriously. We must always think before we act. Always try to see what the consequences of your actions could be before acting in a manner that could set some one off. We need to start letting things go.

It is time we understand we all have differences and learn to accept them. Don't let everything become a major issue. If we see someone park in a handicap parking space, we all know it's wrong, but we don't need to react to it or say something to the person. Let karma work in its own wonderful way. If you let it go when you come out of the story you may very well see them getting a parking ticket or having their car towed.

If someone in front of you has too many items in the express lane let it slide. There may be a reason the yare in rush like a medical or other emergency, the store personnel themselves may something or you may be in the same situation some day you just never know. Yes, rules are made for a reason but some one is always going to break those rules, it is not worth losing sleep over.

Next let's all try to have manners and respect of each other. Hold a door for someone even if they find it offensive that's on them not you. Say thank you occasionally or just tell someone they are doing a great job, you may very well make their day. Especially if they were having a bad day you very well change that for them. Do a few good deeds now and then, not because you expect a reward but just because it is the right thing to do. Never do something because you expect a reward, do it because it's the right thing to do. Try to pay it forward as well. Sometimes people will do nice things because it makes them feel good. Be like those people, pay for some one else's order, mow your neighbor's lawn, volunteer for an organization, put money in the charity bucket at a store or just do something nice for your spouse. The feeling you get will out weigh any other reward you could ever receive.

Finally take some time to detach, no not from reality but from the every day stressors in life. Take day off from politics, it doesn't need to be the main topic of our life. We must not let politic rue the day. Take some time and read a good book, reconnect with your spouse or old friends. Or even take your family on a day trip. Many city libraries offer free passes to museums and other activities so saying you can't afford it isn't a valid excuse. Unless you're a fitness buff or go to the gym daily we could all use some more exercise. Go for a walk or a hike, take a swim in the pool or lake or even just go to the mall and look around. Next must of us push ourselves harder than we need to at times. Occasionally take a nap or get an extra hour sleep it will do wonders for you. Once awhile we also need to detach from technology, take a day off from the internet and social media in order to allow you to clear your mind. Just sit out side once a while and listen to the sounds of nature you will find it quite relaxing.

One last bit of advice I can offer you is to stop the bad habits you take part in. Try to quit smoking or drinking or other things that don't serve you or your health very well. We all know this isn't easy so don't set yourself up for failure. Take baby steps at first maybe cutdown 1 drink or reduce how much you smoke per day. It all comes down to putting one foot in front of the other. We can only take one step at a time but as we do, we build a foundation and head in the right direction. Just like Neil Armstrong said it will be one small step for man but will eventually lead to one giant leap for mankind.

The Democratic Asylum

Preamble to the Bill of Rights

*Congress of the United States

begun and held at the City of New-York,
on Wednesday the fourth of March one thousand
seven hundred and eighty-nine.

THE Conventions of several the States, having at
the time of their adopting the Constitution,
expressed a desire, in order to prevent
misconstruction or abuse of its powers, that further
declaratory and restrictive clauses should be added:
And as extending the ground of public confidence
in the Government, will best ensure the beneficent
ends of its institution. RESOLVED by the Senate
and House of Representatives of the United States
of America, in Congress assembled, two thirds of
both Houses concurring, that the following Articles
be proposed to the Legislatures of the several
States, as amendments to the Constitution of the
United States, all, or any of which Articles, when
ratified by three fourths of the said Legislatures, to
be valid to all intents and purposes, as part of the
said Constitution; viz. ARTICLES in addition to,
and Amendment of the Constitution of the United
States of America, proposed by Congress, and
ratified by the Legislatures of the several States,
pursuant to the fifth Article of the original
Constitution.

Frederick Augustus Muhlenberg Speaker of the
House of Representatives John Adams, Vice-

President of the United States and President of the Senate.

Attest, John Beckley, Clerk of the House of Representatives. Sam. A. Otis Secretary of the Senate. *On September 25, 1789, Congress transmitted to the state legislatures twelve proposed amendments, two of which, having to do with Congressional representation and Congressional pay, were not adopted. The remaining ten amendments became the Bill of Rights.

Amendment 1

- Freedom of Religion, Speech, and the Press

Congress shall make no law respecting an establishment of religion or prohibiting the free exercise thereof or abridging the freedom of speech or of the press, or the right of the people peaceably to assemble and to petition the government for a redress of grievances.

Amendment 2

- The Right to Bear Arms

A well-regulated Militia being necessary to the security of a free State, the right of the people to keep and bear Arms shall not be infringed.

Amendment 3
- The Housing of Soldiers

No soldier shall, in time of peace, be quartered in any house without the consent of the owner, nor in time of war but in a manner to be prescribed by law.

Amendment 4
- Protection from Unreasonable Searches and Seizures

The right of the people to be secure in their persons, houses, papers, and effects against unreasonable searches and seizure shall not be violated, and no warrants shall issue but upon probable cause, supported by oath or affirmation, and particularly describing the place to be searched and the persons or things to be seized.

Amendment 5
- Protection of Rights to Life, Liberty, and Property

No person shall be held to answer for a capital or otherwise infamous crime unless on a presentment or indictment of a grand jury, except in cases arising in the land or naval forces, or in the militia, when in actual service in time of war or public danger; nor shall any person be subject for the same offense to be twice put in jeopardy of life or limb; nor shall be compelled in any criminal case to be a witness against himself, nor be deprived of life, liberty, or property without due process of law; nor shall private property be taken for public use without just compensation.

Amendment 6

- Rights of Accused Persons in Criminal Cases
In all criminal prosecutions, the accused shall enjoy the right to a speedy and public trial by an impartial jury of the state and district wherein the crime shall have been committed, which district shall have been previously ascertained by law, and to be informed of the nature and cause of the accusation; to be confronted with the witnesses against him; to have compulsory process for obtaining witnesses in his favor; and to have the assistance of counsel for his defense.

Amendment 7

- Rights in Civil Cases
In suits at common law, where the value in controversy shall exceed twenty dollars, the right of trial by jury shall be preserved, and no fact tried by a jury shall be otherwise reexamined in any court of

the United States than according to the rules of the common law.

Amendment 8
- Excessive Bail, Fines, and Punishments Forbidden
Excessive bail shall not be required, nor excessive fines imposed, nor cruel and unusual punishments inflicted.

Amendment 9
- Other Rights Kept by the People
The enumeration in the Constitution of certain rights shall not be construed to deny or disparage others retained by the people.

Amendment 10
- Undelegated Powers Kept by the States and the People
The powers not delegated to the United States by the Constitution, nor prohibited by it to the states, are reserved to the states respectively, or to the people

ABOUT THE AUTHOR

Keith M Rauh, was born in and is a lifelong resident of the liberal utopia of Massachusetts. He was raised by a traditional two parent family and has one brother. He subscribes to both conservative and liberal views depending on the issue. He received Ged in 1992 and attended one year of college before following other interests. Mr. Rauh lives with Asperger's syndrome an autism spectrum disorder, adhd and several mental health conditions including anxiety, panic attacks. He also deals with several physical ailments including hearing loss, tinnitus and chronic fatigues. Despite all this he pushes hard to do as much as he possibly can daily. He is married and has three children of which two are now adults and one is a teen ager. He has worked in many career fields including food service, manufacturing, and transportation. He ran his own small business with his wife for ten years. His latest adventure is hosting the Trumped-up podcast.

United we stand, divide we fall.

Check out the trumped up podcast @

Anchor.fm/keith-rauh

You can follow us on face book, twitter, Instagram and you tube

All in all, it's just another brick in the wall (pink Floyd)

My family is the greatest inspiration ever!

MAKE SURE YOU VOTE!